PENGUIN PLAYS

INCIDENT AT VICHY

Arthur Miller was born in New York City in 1915 and studied at the University of Michigan. His plays include *All My Sons* (1947), *Death of a Salesman* (1949), *The Crucible* (1953), *A View from the Bridge* and *A Memory of Two Mondays* (1955), *After the Fall* (1963), *Incident at Vichy* (1964), *The Price* (1968), *The Creation of the World and Other Business* (1972), and *The American Clock* (1980). He has also written two novels, *Focus* (1945), and *The Misfits*, which was filmed in 1960, and the text for *In Russia* (1969), *Chinese Encounters* (1979), and *In the Country* (1977), three books of photographs by his wife, Inge Morath. His most recent works include a memoir, *Timebends* (1987), and the plays, *The Ride Down Mt. Morgan* (1991), *The Last Yankee* (1993), *Broken Glass* (1933), which won the Olivier Award for Best Play of the London Season, and *Mr. Peters' Connections* (1998). He has twice won the New York Drama Critics Circle Award, and in 1949 he was awarded the Pulitzer Prize.

BY ARTHUR MILLER

DRAMA

The Golden Years
The Man Who Had All the Luck
All My Sons
Death of a Salesman
An Enemy of the People (*adaptation of the play by Ibsen*)
The Crucible
A View from the Bridge
After the Fall
Incident at Vichy
The Price
The American Clock
The Creation of the World and Other Business
The Archbishop's Ceiling
The Ride Down Mt. Morgan
Broken Glass
Mr. Peters' Connections

ONE-ACT PLAYS

A View from the Bridge, *one-act version, with* A Memory of Two Mondays
Elegy for a Lady (*in* Two-Way Mirror)
Some Kind of Love Story (*in* Two-Way Mirror)
I Can't Remember Anything (*in* Danger: Memory!)
Clara (*in* Danger: Memory!)
The Last Yankee

OTHER WORKS

Situation Normal
The Misfits (*a cinema novel*)
Focus (*a novel*)
I Don't Need You Anymore (*short stories*)
Theatre Essays
Chinese Encounters (*reportage with Inge Morath photographs*)
In the Country (*reportage with Inge Morath photographs*)
In Russia (*reportage with Inge Morath photographs*)
Salesman in Beijing (*a memoir*)
Timebends (*autobiography*)
Homely Girl, A Life (*novella*)

COLLECTIONS

Arthur Miller's Collected Plays (Volumes I and II)
The Portable Arthur Miller
The Theater Essays of Arthur Miller (*Robert Martin, editor*)

VIKING CRITICAL LIBRARY EDITIONS

Death of a Salesman (*edited by Gerald Weales*)
The Crucible (*edited by Gerald Weales*)

TELEVISION

Playing for Time

SCREENPLAYS

The Misfits
Everybody Wins
The Crucible

INCIDENT AT VICHY

A PLAY

ARTHUR MILLER

PENGUIN BOOKS

PENGUIN BOOKS
Published by the Penguin Group
Penguin Books USA Inc.,
375 Hudson Street, New York, New York 10014, U.S.A.
Penguin Books Ltd, 27 Wrights Lane, London W8 5TZ, England
Penguin Books Australia Ltd, Ringwood, Victoria, Australia
Penguin Books Canada Ltd, 10 Alcorn Avenue,
Toronto, Ontario, Canada M4V 3B2
Penguin Books (N.Z.) Ltd, 182-190 Wairau Road, Auckland 10, New Zealand

Penguin Books Ltd, Registered Offices:
Harmondsworth, Middlesex, England

First published in the United States of America by Viking Penguin Inc. 1965
Reprinted 1966
Published in Penguin Books 1985

9 10

LIBRARY OF CONGRESS CATALOGING IN PUBLICATION DATA
Miller, Arthur, 1915–
Incident at Vichy.
Originally published: New York: Viking, 1965.
1. World War, 1939–1945—Drama. I. Title.
PS3525.I515615   1985   812'.52   84-26556
ISBN 0 14 048.193 1

Printed in the United States of America
Set in Times Roman

For Robert

INCIDENT AT VICHY

Characters

LEBEAU, a painter

BAYARD, an electrician

MARCHAND, a businessman

POLICE GUARD

MONCEAU, an actor

GYPSY

WAITER

BOY

MAJOR

FIRST DETECTIVE

OLD JEW

SECOND DETECTIVE

LEDUC, a doctor

POLICE CAPTAIN

VON BERG, a Prince

PROFESSOR HOFFMAN

FERRAND, a café proprietor

FOUR PRISONERS

Vichy, France, 1942. A place of detention.

At the right a corridor leads to a turning and an unseen door to the street. Across the back is a structure with two grimy window panes in it—perhaps an office, in any case a private room with a door opening from it at the left.

A long bench stands in front of this room, facing a large empty area whose former use is unclear but which suggests a warehouse, perhaps, an armory, or part of a railroad station not used by the public. Two small boxes stand apart on either side of the bench.

When light begins to rise, six men and a boy of fifteen are discovered on the bench in attitudes expressive of their personalities and functions, frozen there like members of a small orchestra at the moment before they begin to play.

As normal light comes on, their positions flow out of the frieze. It appears that they do not know one another and are sitting like people thrown together in a public place, mutually curious but self-occupied. However, they are anxious and frightened and tend to make themselves small and unobtrusive. Only one, Marchand, a fairly well-dressed businessman, keeps glancing at his watch and bits of paper and calling

cards he keeps in his pockets, and seems normally im-
patient.

Now, out of hunger and great anxiety, Lebeau, a
bearded, unkempt man of twenty-five, lets out a dram-
atized blow of air and leans forward to rest his head
on his hands. Others glance at him, then away. He is
charged with the energy of fear, and it makes him
seem aggressive.

LEBEAU: Cup of coffee would be nice. Even a sip.

No one responds. He turns to Bayard beside him;
Bayard is his age, poorly but cleanly dressed, with a
certain muscular austerity in his manner. Lebeau
speaks in a private undertone.

You wouldn't have any idea what's going on, would you?

BAYARD, *shaking his head*: I was walking down the street.

LEBEAU: Me too. Something told me—Don't go outside today. So I went out. Weeks go by and I don't open my door.
Today I go out. And I had no reason, I wasn't even going
anywhere. *Looks left and right to the others. To Bayard*: They
get picked up the same way?

BAYARD—*shrugs*: I've only been here a couple of minutes
myself—just before they brought you in.

LEBEAU—*looks to the others*: Does anybody know anything?

They shrug and shake their heads. Lebeau looks at the
walls, the room; then he speaks to Bayard.

This isn't a police station, is it?

BAYARD: Doesn't seem so. There's always a desk. It's just
some building they're using, I guess.

LEBEAU, *glancing about uneasily, curiously*: It's painted like a police station, though. There must be an international police paint, they're always the same color everywhere. Like dead clams, and a little yellow mixed in.

> *Pause. He glances at the other silent men, and tries to silence himself, like them. But it's impossible, and he speaks to Bayard with a nervous smile.*

You begin wishing you'd committed a crime, you know? Something definite.

BAYARD—*he is not amused, but not unsympathetic*: Try to take it easy. It's no good getting excited. We'll find out soon.

LEBEAU: It's just that I haven't eaten since three o'clock yesterday afternoon. Everything gets more vivid when you're hungry—you ever notice that?

BAYARD: I'd give you something, but I forgot my lunch this morning. Matter of fact, I was just turning back to get it when they came up alongside me. Whyn't you try to sit back and relax?

LEBEAU: I'm nervous. . . . I mean I'm nervous anyway. *With a faint, frightened laugh*: I was even nervous before the war.

> *His little smile vanishes. He shifts in his seat. The others wait with subdued anxiety. He notices the good clothes and secure manner of Marchand, who is at the head of the line, nearest the door. He leans forward to attract him.*

Excuse me.

> *Marchand does not turn to him. He gives a short, sharp, low whistle. Marchand, already offended, turns slowly to him.*

Is that the way they picked you up? On the street?

> *Marchand turns forward again without answering.*

Sir?

> *Marchand still does not turn back to him.*

Well, Jesus, pardon me for living.

MARCHAND: It's perfectly obvious they're making a routine identity check.

LEBEAU: Oh.

MARCHAND: With so many strangers pouring into Vichy this past year there're probably a lot of spies and God knows what. It's just a document check, that's all.

LEBEAU—*turns to Bayard, hopefully*: You think so?

BAYARD—*shrugs; obviously he feels there is something more to it*: I don't know.

MARCHAND, *to Bayard*: Why? There are thousands of people running around with false papers, we all know that. You can't permit such things in wartime.

> *The others glance uneasily at Marchand, whose sense of security is thereby confined to him alone.*

Especially now with the Germans starting to take over down here you have to expect things to be more strict, it's inevitable.

> *A pause. Lebeau once again turns to him.*

LEBEAU: You don't get any . . . special flavor, huh?

MARCHAND: What flavor?

LEBEAU, *glancing at the others*: Well like . . . some racial . . . implication?

MARCHAND: I don't see anything to fear if your papers are all right. *He turns front, concluding the conversation.*

> *Again silence. But Lebeau can't contain his anxiety. He studies Bayard's profile, then turns to the man on his other side and studies his. Then, turning back to Bayard, he speaks quietly.*

LEBEAU: Listen, you are . . . Peruvian, aren't you?

BAYARD: What's the matter with you, asking questions like that in here? *He turns forward.*

LEBEAU: What am I supposed to do, sit here like a dumb beast?

BAYARD, *laying a calming hand on his knee*: Friend, it's no good getting hysterical.

LEBEAU: I think we've had it. I think all the Peruvians have had it in Vichy. *Suppressing a shout*: In 1939 I had an American visa. Before the invasion. I actually had it in my hand. . . .

BAYARD: Calm down—this may all be routine.

> *Slight pause. Then . . .*

LEBEAU: Listen . . .

> *He leans in and whispers into Bayard's ear. Bayard glances toward Marchand, then shrugs to Lebeau.*

BAYARD: I don't know, maybe; maybe he's not.

LEBEAU, *desperately attempting familiarity*: What about you?

BAYARD: Will you stop asking idiotic questions? You're making yourself ridiculous.

LEBEAU: But I am ridiculous, aren't you? In 1939 we were packed for America. Suddenly my mother wouldn't leave the furniture. I'm here because of a brass bed and some fourth-rate crockery. And a stubborn, ignorant woman.

BAYARD: Yes, but it's not all that simple. You should try to think of why things happen. It helps to know the meaning of one's suffering.

LEBEAU: What meaning? If my mother—

BAYARD: It's not your mother. The monopolies got control of Germany. Big business is out to make slaves of everyone, that's why you're here.

LEBEAU: Well I'm not a philosopher, but I know my mother, and that's why I'm here. You're like people who look at my paintings—"What does this mean, what does that mean?" *Look* at it, don't ask what it means; you're not God, you can't tell what anything means. I'm walking down the street before, a car pulls up beside me, a man gets out and measures my nose, my ears, my mouth, the next thing I'm sitting in a police station—or whatever the hell this is here—and in the middle of Europe, the highest peak of civilization! And you know what it means? After the Romans and the Greeks and the Renaissance, and you know what this means?

BAYARD: You're talking utter confusion.

LEBEAU, *in terror*: Because I'm utterly confused! *He suddenly springs up and shouts*: Goddammit, I want some coffee!

> *The Police Guard appears at the end of the corridor, a revolver on his hip; he strolls down the corridor and meets Lebeau, who has come halfway up. Lebeau halts, returns to his place on the bench, and sits. The*

Guard starts to turn to go up the corridor when Marchand raises his hand.

MARCHAND: Excuse me, officer, is there a telephone one can use? I have an appointment at eleven o'clock and it's quite . . .

The Guard simply walks up the corridor, turns the corner, and disappears. Lebeau looks toward Marchand and shakes his head, laughing silently.

LEBEAU, *to Bayard, sotto*: Isn't it wonderful? The man is probably on his way to work in a German coal mine and he's worried about breaking an appointment. And people want realistic painting, you see what I mean? *Slight pause.* Did they measure your nose? Could you at least tell me that?

BAYARD: No, they just stopped me and asked for my papers. I showed them and they took me in.

MONCEAU, *leaning forward to address Marchand*: I agree with you, sir.

Marchand turns to him. Monceau is a bright-eyed, cheerful man of twenty-eight. His clothes were elegant, now frayed. He holds a gray felt hat on his knee, his posture rather elegant.

Vichy must be full of counterfeit papers. I think as soon as they start, it shouldn't take long. *To Lebeau*: Try to settle down.

LEBEAU, *to Monceau*: Did they measure your nose?

MONCEAU, *disapprovingly*: I think it'd be best if we all kept quiet.

LEBEAU: What is it, my clothes? How do you know, I might be the greatest painter in France.

MONCEAU: For your sake, I hope you are.

LEBEAU: What a crew! I mean the animosity!

Pause.

MARCHAND, *leaning forward to see Monceau*: You would think, though, that with the manpower shortage they'd economize on personnel. In the car that stopped me there was a driver, two French detectives, and a German official of some kind. They could easily have put a notice in the paper—everyone would have come here to present his documents. This way it's a whole morning wasted. Aside from the embarrassment.

LEBEAU: I'm not embarrassed, I'm scared to death. *To Bayard*: You embarrassed?

BAYARD: Look, if you can't be serious just leave me alone.

> *Pause. Lebeau leans forward to see the man sitting on the far side of Marchand. He points.*

LEBEAU: Gypsy?

GYPSY, *drawing closer a copper pot at his feet*: Gypsy.

LEBEAU, *to Monceau*: Gypsies never have papers. Why'd they bother him?

MONCEAU: In his case it might be some other reason. He probably stole that pot.

GYPSY: No. On the sidewalk. *He raises the pot from between his feet.* I fix, make nice. I sit down to fix. Come police. Pfft!

MARCHAND: But of course they'll tell you anything. . . . *To Gypsy, laughing familiarly*: Right?

> *Gypsy laughs and turns away to his own gloom.*

LEBEAU: That's a hell of a thing to say to him. I mean, would you say that to a man with pressed pants?

MARCHAND: They don't mind. In fact, they're proud of stealing. *To Gypsy:* Aren't you?

> *Gypsy glances at him, shrugs.*

I've got a place in the country where they come every summer. I like them, personally—especially the music. *With a broad grin he sings toward the Gypsy and laughs.* We often listen to them around their campfires. But they'll steal the eyes out of your head. *To Gypsy:* Right?

> *Gypsy shrugs and kisses the air contemptuously. Marchand laughs with brutal familiarity.*

LEBEAU: Why shouldn't he steal? How'd you get *your* money?

MARCHAND: I happen to be in business.

LEBEAU: So what have you got against stealing?

BAYARD: Are you trying to provoke somebody? Is that it?

LEBEAU: Another businessman.

BAYARD: I happen to be an electrician. But a certain amount of solidarity wouldn't hurt right now.

LEBEAU: How about some solidarity with Gypsies? Just because they don't work nine to five?

WAITER—*a small man, middle-aged, still wearing his apron*: I know this one. I've made him go away a hundred times. He and his wife stand outside the café with a baby, and they beg. It's not even their baby.

LEBEAU: So what? They've still got a little imagination.

WAITER: Yes, but they keep whining to the customers through the shrubbery. People don't like it.

LEBEAU: You know—you all remind me of my father. Always worshiped the hard-working Germans. And now you hear it all over France—we have to learn how to work like the Germans. Good God, don't you ever read history? Whenever a people starts to work hard, watch out, they're going to kill somebody.

BAYARD: That depends on how production is organized. If it's for private profit, yes, but—

LEBEAU: What are you talking about, when did the Russians start getting dangerous? When they learned how to work. Look at the Germans—for a thousand years peaceful, disorganized people—they start working and they're on everybody's back. Nobody's afraid of the Africans, are they? Because they don't work. Read the Bible—work is a curse, you're not supposed to worship work.

MARCHAND: And how do you propose to produce anything?

LEBEAU: Well that's the problem.

Marchand and Bayard laugh.

What are you laughing at? *That is the problem!* Yes! To work without making work a god! What kind of crew is this?

The office door opens and the Major comes out. He is twenty-eight, a wan but well-built man; there is something ill about him. He walks with a slight limp, passing the line of men as he goes toward the corridor.

WAITER: Good morning, Major.

MAJOR—*startled, nods to the Waiter*: Oh. Good morning. *He continues up the corridor, where he summons the Guard around the corner—the Guard appears and they talk unheard.*

MARCHAND, *sotto*: You know him?

WAITER, *proudly*: I serve him breakfast every morning. Tell you the truth, he's really not a bad fellow. Regular army, see, not one of these S.S. bums. Got wounded somewhere, so they stuck him back here. Only came about a month ago, but he and I—

> *The Major comes back down the corridor. The Guard returns to his post out of sight at the corridor's end. As the Major passes Marchand . . .*

MARCHAND, *leaping up and going to the Major*: Excuse me, sir.

> *The Major slowly turns his face to Marchand. Marchand affects to laugh deferentially.*

I hate to trouble you, but I would be much obliged if I could use a telephone for one minute. In fact, it's business connected to the food supply. I am the manager of . . .

> *He starts to take out a business card, but the Major has turned away and walks to the door. But there he stops and turns back.*

MAJOR: I'm not in charge of this procedure. You will have to wait for the Captain of Police. *He goes into the office.*

MARCHAND: I beg your pardon.

> *The door has been closed on his line. He goes back to his place and sits, glaring at the Waiter.*

WAITER: He's not a really bad fellow.

They all look at him, eager for some clue.

He even comes at night sometimes, plays a beautiful piano. Gives himself French lessons out of a book. Always has a few nice words to say, too.

LEBEAU: Does he know that you're a . . . Peruvian?

BAYARD, *instantly*: Don't discuss that here, for God's sake! What's the matter with you?

LEBEAU: Can't I find out what's going on? If it's a general identity check it's one thing, but if—

> *From the end of the corridor enter First Detective with the Old Jew, a man in his seventies, bearded, carrying a large sackcloth bundle; then the Second Detective, holding the arm of Leduc; then the Police Captain, uniformed, with Von Berg; and finally the Professor in civilian clothes.*
>
> *The First Detective directs the Old Jew to sit, and he does, beside the Gypsy. The Second Detective directs Von Berg to sit beside the Old Jew. Only now does the Second Detective release his hold on Leduc and indicate that he is to sit beside Von Berg.*

SECOND DETECTIVE, *to Leduc*: Don't you give me any more trouble now.

> *The door opens and the Major enters. Instantly Leduc is on his feet, approaching the Major.*

LEDUC: Sir, I must ask the reason for this. I am a combat officer, captain in the French Army. There is no authority to arrest me in French territory. The Occupation has not revoked French law in southern France.

The Second Detective, infuriated, throws Leduc back into his seat. He returns to the Professor.

SECOND DETECTIVE, *to Major, of Leduc*: Speechmaker.

PROFESSOR, *doubtfully*: You think you two can carry on now?

SECOND DETECTIVE: We got the idea, Professor. *To the Major*: There's certain neighborhoods they head for when they run away from Paris or wherever they come from. I can get you as many as you can handle.

FIRST DETECTIVE: It's a question of knowing the neighborhoods, you see. In my opinion you've got at least a couple thousand in Vichy on false papers.

PROFESSOR: You go ahead, then.

As the Second Detective turns to go with the First Detective, the Police Captain calls him.

CAPTAIN: Saint-Père.

SECOND DETECTIVE: Yes sir.

The Captain walks downstage with the Detective.

CAPTAIN: Try to avoid taking anybody out of a crowd. Just cruise around the way we did before, and take them one at a time. There are all kinds of rumors. We don't want to alarm people.

SECOND DETECTIVE: Right, sir.

The Captain gestures, and both Detectives leave up the corridor.

CAPTAIN: I am just about to order coffee. Will you gentlemen have some?

PROFESSOR: Please.

WAITER, *timidly*: And a croissant for the Major.

> *The Major glances quickly at the Waiter and barely smiles. The Captain, who has thrown a mystified look at the Waiter, goes into the office.*

MARCHAND, *to the Professor*: I believe I am first, sir.

PROFESSOR: Yes, this way.

> *He goes into the office, followed by the eager Marchand.*

MARCHAND, *going in*: Thank you. I'm in a dreadful hurry. . . . I was on my way to the Ministry of Supply, in fact. . . .

> *His voice is lost within. As the Major reaches the door, Leduc, who has been in a fever of calculation, calls to him.*

LEDUC: Amiens.

MAJOR—*he halts at the door, turns to Leduc, who is at the far end of the line*: What about Amiens?

LEDUC, *suppressing his nervousness*: June ninth, 'forty. I was in the Sixteenth Artillery, facing you. I recognize your insignia, which of course I could hardly forget.

MAJOR: That was a bad day for you fellows.

LEDUC: Yes. And evidently for you.

MAJOR—*glances down at his leg*: Can't complain.

> *The Major goes into the office, shuts the door. A pause.*

LEDUC, *to all*: What's this all about?

WAITER, *to all*: I told you he wasn't a bad guy. You'll see.

MONCEAU, *to Leduc*: It seems they're checking on identification papers.

> *Leduc receives the news, and obviously grows cautious and quietly alarmed. He examines their faces.*

LEDUC: What's the procedure?

MONCEAU: They've just started—that businessman was the first.

LEBEAU, *to Leduc and Von Berg*: They measure your noses?

LEDUC, *sharply alarmed*: Measure noses?

LEBEAU, *putting thumb and forefinger against the bridge and tip of his nose*: Ya, they measured my nose, right on the street. I tell you what I think . . . *To Bayard*: With your permission.

BAYARD: I don't mind you talking as long as you're serious.

LEBEAU: I think it's to carry stones. It just occurred to me —last Monday a girl I know came up from Marseille— the road is full of detours. They probably need labor. She said there was a crowd of people just carrying stones. Lot of them Jews, she thought; hundreds.

LEDUC: I never heard of forced labor in the Vichy Zone. Is that going on here?

BAYARD: Where do you come from?

LEDUC—*slight pause—he decides whether to reveal*: I live in the country. I don't get into town very often. There's been no forced-labor decree, has there?

BAYARD, *to all*: Now, listen. *Everyone turns to his straightforward, certain tone.* I'm going to tell you something, but I don't want anybody quoting me. Is that understood?

> *They nod. He glances at the door. He turns to Lebeau.*

You hear what I said?

LEBEAU: Don't make me out some kind of an idiot. Christ's sake, I know it's serious!

BAYARD, *to the others*: I work in the railroad yards. A thirty-car freight train pulled in yesterday. The engineer is Polish, so I couldn't talk to him, but one of the switchmen says he heard people inside.

LEDUC: Inside the cars?

BAYARD: Yes. It came from Toulouse. I heard there's been a quiet roundup of Jews in Toulouse the last couple of weeks. And what's a Polish engineer doing on a train in southern France? You understand?

LEDUC: Concentration camp?

MONCEAU: Why? A lot of people have been volunteering for work in Germany. That's no secret. They're doubling the ration for anybody who goes.

BAYARD, *quietly*: The cars are locked on the outside. *Slight pause.* And they stink. You can smell the stench a hundred yards away. Babies are crying inside. You can hear them. And women. They don't lock volunteers in that way. I never heard of it.

> *A long pause.*

LEDUC: But I've never heard of them applying the Racial Laws down here. It's still French territory, regardless of the Occupation—they've made a big point of that.

Pause.

BAYARD: The Gypsy bothers me.

LEBEAU: Why?

BAYARD: They're in the same category of the Racial Laws. Inferior.

> *Leduc and Lebeau slowly turn to look at the Gypsy.*

LEBEAU, *turning back quickly to Bayard*: Unless he really stole that pot.

BAYARD: Well, yes, if he stole the pot then of course he—

LEBEAU, *quickly, to the Gypsy*: Hey, listen. *He gives a soft, sharp whistle. The Gypsy turns to him.* You steal that pot?

> *The Gypsy's face is inscrutable. Lebeau is embar-*
> *rassed to press this, and more desperate.*

You did, didn't you?

GYPSY: No steal, no.

LEBEAU: Look, I've got nothing against stealing. *Indicating the others*: I'm not one of these types. I've slept in parked cars, under bridges—I mean, to me all property is theft anyway so I've got no prejudice against you.

GYPSY: No steal.

LEBEAU: Look . . . I mean you're a Gypsy, so how else can you live, right?

WAITER: He steals everything.

LEBEAU, *to Bayard*: You hear? He's probably in for stealing, that's all.

VON BERG: Excuse me . . .

> *They turn to him.*

Have you all been arrested for being Jewish?

> *They are silent, suspicious and surprised.*

I'm terribly sorry. I had no idea.

BAYARD: I said nothing about being Jewish. As far as I know, nobody here is Jewish.

VON BERG: I'm terribly sorry.

> *Silence. The moment lengthens. In his embarrassment he laughs nervously.*

It's only that I . . . I was buying a newspaper and this gentleman came out of a car and told me I must have my documents checked. I . . . I had no idea.

> *Silence. Hope is rising in them.*

LEBEAU, *to Bayard*: So what'd they grab *him* for?

BAYARD—*looks at Von Berg for a moment, then addresses all*: I don't understand it, but take my advice. If anything like that happens and you find yourself on that train . . . there are four bolts halfway up the doors on the inside. Try to pick up a nail or a screwdriver, even a sharp stone—you can chisel the wood out around those bolts and the doors will open. I warn you, don't believe anything they tell you —I heard they're working Jews to death in the Polish camps.

MONCEAU: I happen to have a cousin; they sent him to Auschwitz; that's in Poland, you know. I have several letters from him saying he's fine. They've even taught him bricklaying.

BAYARD: Look, friend, I'm telling you what I heard from people who know. *Hesitates.* People who make it their business to know, you understand? Don't listen to any stories about resettlement, or that they're going to teach you a trade or something. If you're on that train get out before it gets where it's going.

> *Pause.*

LEDUC: I've heard the same thing.

> *They turn to him and he turns to Bayard.*

How would one find tools, you have any idea?

MONCEAU: This is so typical! We're in the French Zone, nobody has said one word to us, and we're already on a train for a concentration camp where we'll be dead in a year.

LEDUC: But if the engineer is a Pole . . .

MONCEAU: So he's a Pole, what does that prove?

BAYARD: All I'm saying is that if you have some kind of tool . . .

LEDUC: I think what this man says should be taken seriously.

MONCEAU: In my opinion you're hysterical. After all, they were picking up Jews in Germany for years before the war, they've been doing it in Paris since they came in—are you telling me all those people are dead? Is that really conceivable to you? War is war, but you still have to keep a certain sense of proportion. I mean Germans are still *people*.

LEDUC: I don't speak this way because they're Germans.

BAYARD: It's that they're Fascists.

LEDUC: Excuse me, no. It's exactly because they are people that I speak this way.

BAYARD: I don't agree with *that*.

MONCEAU—*looks at Leduc for an instant*: You must have had a peculiar life, is all I can say. I happen to have played in Germany; I know the German people.

LEDUC: I studied in Germany for five years, and in Austria and I—

VON BERG, *happily*: In Austria! Where?

LEDUC—*again he hesitates, then reveals*: The Psychoanalytic Institute in Vienna.

VON BERG: Imagine!

MONCEAU: You're a psychiatrist. *To the others*: No wonder he's so pessimistic!

VON BERG: Where did you live? I am Viennese.

LEDUC: Excuse me, but perhaps it would be wiser not to speak in . . . detail.

VON BERG, *glancing about as though he had committed a gaffe*: I'm terribly sorry . . . yes, of course. *Slight pause.* I was only curious if you knew Baron Kessler. He was very interested in the medical school.

LEDUC, *with an odd coolness*: No, I was never in that circle.

VON BERG: Oh, but he is extremely democratic. He . . . *shyly*: he is my cousin, you see. . . .

LEBEAU: You're a nobleman?

VON BERG: Yes.

LEDUC: What is your name?

VON BERG: Wilhelm Johann Von Berg.

MONCEAU, *astonished, impressed*: The prince?

VON BERG: Yes . . . forgive me, have we met?

MONCEAU, *excited by the honor*: Oh, no. But naturally I've heard your name. I believe it's one of the oldest houses in Austria.

VON BERG: Oh, that's of no importance any more.

LEBEAU, *turning to Bayard—bursting with hope*: Now, what the hell would they want with an Austrian prince?

> *Bayard looks at Von Berg, mystified.*

I mean . . . *Turning back to Von Berg*: You're Catholic, right?

VON BERG: Yes.

LEDUC: But is your title on your papers?

VON BERG: Oh, yes, my passport.

> *Pause. They sit silent, on the edge of hope, but bewildered.*

BAYARD: Were you . . . political or something?

VON BERG: No, no, I never had any interest in that direction. *Slight pause.* Of course, there is this resentment toward the nobility. That might explain it.

LEDUC: In the Nazis? Resentment?

VON BERG, *surprised*: Yes, certainly.

LEDUC, *with no evident viewpoint but with a neutral but pressing interest in drawing the nobleman out*: Really. I've never been aware of that.

VON BERG: Oh, I assure you.

LEDUC: But on what ground?

VON BERG—*laughs, embarrassed to have to even suggest he is offended*: You're not asking that seriously.

LEDUC: Don't be offended, I'm simply ignorant of that situation. I suppose I have taken for granted that the aristocracy is . . . always behind a reactionary regime.

VON BERG: Oh, there are some, certainly. But for the most part they never took responsibility, in any case.

LEDUC: That interests me. So you still take seriously the . . . the title and . . .

VON BERG: It is not a "title"; it is my name, my family. Just as you have a name, and a family. And you are not inclined to dishonor them, I presume.

LEDUC: I see. And by responsibility, you mean, I suppose, that—

VON BERG: Oh, I don't know; whatever that means. *He glances at his watch.*

> *Pause.*

LEDUC: Please forgive me, I didn't mean to pry into your affairs. *Pause.* I'd never thought about it, but it's obvious now—they *would* want to destroy whatever power you have.

VON BERG: Oh, no, I have no power. And if I did it would be a day's work for them to destroy it. That's not the issue.

> *Pause.*

LEDUC, *fascinated—he is drawn to some truth in Von Berg*: What is it, then? Believe me, I'm not being critical. Quite the contrary . . .

VON BERG: But these are obvious answers! *He laughs.* I have a certain . . . standing. My name is a thousand years old, and they know the danger if someone like me is perhaps . . . not vulgar enough.

LEDUC: And by vulgar you mean . . .

VON BERG: Well, don't you think Nazism . . . whatever else it may be . . . is an outburst of vulgarity? An ocean of vulgarity?

BAYARD: I'm afraid it's a lot more than that, my friend.

VON BERG, *politely, to Bayard*: I am sure it is, yes.

BAYARD: You make it sound like they have bad table manners, that's all.

VON BERG: They certainly do, yes. Nothing angers them more than a sign of any . . . refinement. It is decadent, you see.

BAYARD: What kind of statement is that? You mean you left Austria because of their table manners?

VON BERG: Table manners, yes; and their adoration of dreadful art; and grocery clerks in uniform telling the orchestra what music it may not play. Vulgarity can be enough to send a man out of his country, yes, I think so.

BAYARD: In other words, if they had good taste in art, and elegant table manners, and let the orchestra play whatever it liked, they'd be all right with you.

VON BERG: But how would that be possible? Can people with respect for art go about hounding Jews? Making a prison of Europe, pushing themselves forward as a race of policemen and brutes? Is that possible for artistic people?

MONCEAU: I'd like to agree with you, Prince von Berg, but I have to say that the German audiences—I've played there —no audience is as sensitive to the smallest nuance of a performance; they sit in the theater with respect, like in a church. And nobody listens to music like a German. Don't you think so? It's a passion with them.

> *Pause.*

VON BERG, *appalled at the truth*: I'm afraid that is true, yes. *Pause.* I don't know what to say. *He is depressed, deeply at a loss.*

LEDUC: Perhaps it isn't those people who are doing this.

VON BERG: I'm afraid I know many cultivated people who . . . did become Nazis. Yes, they did. Art is perhaps no defense against this. It's curious how one takes certain ideas for granted. Until this moment I had thought of art as a . . . *To Bayard*: You may be right—I don't understand very much about it. Actually, I'm essentially a musician—in an amateur way, of course, and politics has never . . .

> *The office door opens and Marchand appears, backing out, talking to someone within. He is putting a leather document-wallet into his breast pocket, while with the other hand he holds a white pass.*

MARCHAND: That's perfectly all right, I understand perfectly. Good day, gentlemen. *Holding up the pass to them*: I show the pass at the door? Thank you.

Shutting the door, he turns and hurries past the line of prisoners, and, as he passes the Boy . . .

BOY: What'd they ask you, sir?

Marchand turns up the corridor without glancing at the Boy, and as he approaches the end the Guard, hearing him, appears there. He hands the pass to the Guard and goes out. The Guard moves around the turning of the corridor and disappears.

LEBEAU, *half mystified, half hopeful*: I could have sworn he was a Jew! *To Bayard*: Didn't you think so?

Slight pause.

BAYARD—*clearly he did think so*: You have papers, don't you?

LEBEAU: Oh sure, I have good papers. *He takes rumpled documents out of his pants pocket.*

BAYARD: Well, just insist they're valid. Maybe that's what he did.

LEBEAU: I wish you'd take a look at them, will you?

BAYARD: I'm no expert.

LEBEAU: I'd like your opinion, though. You seem to know what's going on. How they look to you?

Bayard quickly hides the papers as the office door opens. The Professor appears and indicates the Gypsy.

PROFESSOR: Next. You. Come with me.

The Gypsy gets up and starts toward him. The Professor indicates the pot in the Gypsy's hand.

You can leave that.

> *The Gypsy hesitates, glances at the pot.*

I said leave it there.

> *The Gypsy puts the pot down on the bench unwillingly.*

GYPSY: Fix. No steal.

PROFESSOR: Go in.

GYPSY, *indicating the pot, warning the others*: That's mine.

> *The Gypsy goes into the office. The Professor follows him in and shuts the door. Bayard takes the pot, bends the handle off, puts it in his pocket, and sets the pot back where it was.*

LEBEAU, *turning back to Bayard, indicating his papers*: What do you think?

BAYARD—*holds a paper up to the light, turns it over, gives it back to Lebeau*: Look good far as I can tell.

MONCEAU: That man did seem Jewish to me. Didn't he to you, Doctor?

LEDUC: I have no idea. Jews are not a race, you know. They can look like anybody.

LEBEAU, *with the joy of near-certainty*: He just probably had good papers. Because I know people have papers, I mean all you have to do is look at them and you know they're phony. But I mean if you have good papers, right?

> *Monceau has meanwhile taken out his papers and is examining them. The Boy does the same with his. Lebeau turns to Leduc.*

That's true, though. My father looks like an Englishman. The trouble is I took after my mother.

Boy, *to Bayard, offering his paper*: Could you look at mine?

BAYARD: I'm no expert, kid. Anyway, don't sit there looking at them like that.

> *Monceau puts his away, as the Boy does. A pause. They wait.*

MONCEAU: I think it's a question of one's credibility—that man just now did carry himself with a certain confidence. . . .

> *The Old Jew begins to pitch forward onto the floor. Von Berg catches him and with the Boy helps him back onto the seat.*

LEBEAU, *with heightened nervousness*: Christ, you'd think they'd shave off their beards. I mean, to walk around with a beard like that in a country like this!

> *Monceau looks at his beard, and Lebeau touches it.*

Well, I just don't waste time shaving, but . . .

VON BERG, *to the Old Jew*: Are you all right, sir?

> *Leduc bends over Von Berg's lap and feels the Old Jew's pulse. Pause. He lets his hand go, and looks toward Lebeau.*

LEDUC: Were you serious? They actually measured your nose?

LEBEAU: With his fingers. That civilian. They called him "professor." *Pause. Then, to Bayard*: I think you're right; it's all a question of your papers. That businessman certainly looked Jewish. . . .

MONCEAU: I'm not so sure now.

LEBEAU, *angrily*: A minute ago you were sure, now suddenly . . . !

MONCEAU: Well, even if he wasn't—it only means it really is a general checkup. On the whole population.

LEBEAU: Hey, that's right too! *Slight pause.* Actually, I'm often taken for a gentile myself. Not that I give a damn but most of the time, I . . . *To Von Berg*: How about you, they measure your nose?

VON BERG: No, they told me to get into the car, that was all.

LEBEAU: Because actually yours looks bigger than mine.

BAYARD: Will you cut that out! Just cut it out, will you?

LEBEAU: Can't I try to find out what I'm in for?

BAYARD: Did you ever think of anything beside yourself? Just because you're an artist? You people demoralize everybody!

LEBEAU, *with unconcealed terror*: What the hell am I supposed to think of? Who're you thinking of?

> *The office door opens. The Police Captain appears, and gestures toward Bayard.*

CAPTAIN: Come inside here.

> *Bayard, trying hard to keep his knees from shaking, stands. Ferrand, a café proprietor, comes hurrying down the corridor with a tray of coffee things covered with a large napkin. He has an apron on.*

Ah, at last!

FERRAND: Sorry, Captain, but for you I had to make some fresh.

CAPTAIN, *as he goes into the office behind Ferrand*: Put it on my desk.

> *The door is closed. Bayard sits, wipes his face. Pause.*

MONCEAU, *to Bayard, quietly*: Would you mind if I made a suggestion?

> *Bayard turns to him, already defensive.*

You looked terribly uncertain of yourself when you stood up just now.

BAYARD, *taking offense*: Me uncertain? You've got the wrong man.

MONCEAU: Please, I'm not criticizing you.

BAYARD: Naturally I'm a little nervous, facing a room full of Fascists like this.

MONCEAU: But that's why one must seem especially self-confident. I'm quite sure that's what got that businessman through so quickly. I've had similar experiences on trains, and even in Paris when they stopped me several times. The important thing is not to look like a victim. Or even to feel like one. They can be very stupid, but they do have a sense for victims; they know when someone has nothing to hide.

LEDUC: But how does one avoid feeling like a victim?

MONCEAU: One must create one's own reality in this world. I'm an actor, we do this all the time. The audience, you know, is very sadistic; it looks for your first sign of weakness. So you must try to think of something that makes you feel self-assured; anything at all. Like the day, perhaps, when your father gave you a compliment, or a teacher was amazed at your cleverness . . . Any thought—*to Bayard*—that makes you feel . . . valuable. After all, you are trying to create an illusion; to make them believe you are who your papers say you are.

LEDUC: That's true, we must not play the part they have written for us. That's very wise. You must have great courage.

MONCEAU: I'm afraid not. But I have talent instead. *To Bayard*: One must show them the face of a man who is right, not a man who is suspect and wrong. They sense the difference.

BAYARD: My friend, you're in a bad way if you have to put on an act to feel your rightness. The bourgeoisie sold France; they let in the Nazis to destroy the French working class. Remember the causes of this war and you've got *real* confidence.

LEDUC: Excepting that the causes of this war keep changing so often.

BAYARD: Not if you understand the economic and political forces.

LEDUC: Still, when Germany attacked us the Communists refused to support France. They pronounced it an imperialist war. Until the Nazis turned against Russia; then in one afternoon it all changed into a sacred battle against tyranny. What confidence can one feel from an understanding that turns upside down in an afternoon?

BAYARD: My friend, without the Red Army standing up to them right now you could forget France for a thousand years!

LEDUC: I agree. But that does not require an understanding of political and economic forces—it is simply faith in the Red Army.

BAYARD: It is faith in the future; and the future is Socialist. And that is what *I* take in there with *me*.

> *To the others*:

I warn you—I've had experience with these types. You'd better ram a viewpoint up your spine or you'll break in half.

LEDUC: I understand. You mean it's important not to feel alone, is that it?

BAYARD: None of us is alone. We're members of history. Some of us don't know it, but you'd better learn it for your own preservation.

LEDUC: That we are . . . symbols.

BAYARD, *uncertain whether to agree*: Yes. Why not? Symbols, yes.

LEDUC: And you feel that helps you. Believe me, I am genuinely interested.

BAYARD: It helps me because it's the truth. What am I to them personally? Do they know me? You react personally to this, they'll turn you into an idiot. You can't make sense of this on a personal basis.

LEDUC: I agree. *Personally*: But the difficulty is—what can one be if not oneself? For example, the thought of torture or something of that sort . . .

BAYARD, *struggling to live his conviction*: Well, it frightens me—of course. But they can't torture the future; it's out of their hands. Man was not made to be the slave of Big Business. Whatever they do, something inside me is laughing. Because they can't win. Impossible. *He has stiffened himself against his rising fear.*

LEDUC: So that in a sense . . . you aren't here. You personally.

BAYARD: In a sense. Why, what's wrong with that?

LEDUC: Nothing; it may be the best way to hold on to oneself. It's only that ordinarily one tries to experience life, to be in spirit where one's body is. For some of us it's difficult to shift gears and go into reverse. But that's not a problem for you.

BAYARD, *solicitously*: You think a man can ever be himself in this society? When millions go hungry and a few live like kings, and whole races are slaves to the stock market—how can you be yourself in such a world? I put in ten hours a day for a few francs, I see people who never bend their backs and they own the planet. . . . How can my spirit be where my body is? I'd have to be an ape.

VON BERG: Then where is your spirit?

BAYARD: In the future. In the day when the working class is master of the world. *That's* my confidence . . . *To Monceau*: Not some borrowed personality.

VON BERG, *wide-eyed, genuinely asking*: But don't you think . . . excuse me. Are not most of the Nazis . . . of the working class?

BAYARD: Well, naturally, with enough propaganda you can confuse anybody.

VON BERG: I see. *Slight pause.* But in that case, how can one have such confidence in them?

BAYARD: Who do you have confidence in, the aristocracy?

VON BERG: Very little. But in certain aristocrats, yes. And in certain common people.

BAYARD: Are you telling me that history is a question of "certain people"? Are we sitting here because we are "certain people"? Is any of us an individual to them? Class interest makes history, not individuals.

VON BERG: Yes. That seems to be the trouble.

BAYARD: Facts are not trouble. A human being has to glory in the facts.

VON BERG, *with a deep, anxious out-reaching to Bayard*: But the facts . . . Dear sir, what if the facts are dreadful? And will always be dreadful?

BAYARD: So is childbirth, so is . . .

VON BERG: But a child comes of it. What if nothing comes of the facts but endless, endless disaster? Believe me, I am happy to meet a man who is not cynical; any faith is precious these days. But to give your faith to a . . . a class of people is impossible, simply impossible—ninety-nine per cent of the Nazis are ordinary working-class people!

BAYARD: I concede it *is* possible to propagandize . . .

VON BERG, *with an untoward anxiety, as though the settlement of this issue is intimate with him*: But what can *not* be propagandized? Isn't that the . . . the only point? A few individuals. Don't you think so?

BAYARD: You're an intelligent man, Prince. Are you seriously telling me that five, ten, a thousand, ten thousand decent people of integrity are all that stand between us and the end of everything? You mean this whole world is going to hang on that thread?

VON BERG, *struck*: I'm afraid it does sound impossible.

BAYARD: If I thought that, I wouldn't have the strength to walk through that door, I wouldn't know how to put one foot in front of the other.

VON BERG—*slight pause*: Yes. I hadn't really considered it that way. But . . . you really think the working class will . . .

BAYARD: They will destroy Fascism because it is against their interest.

VON BERG—*nods*: But in that case, isn't it even more of a mystery?

BAYARD: I see no mystery.

VON BERG: But they adore Hitler.

BAYARD: How can you say that? Hitler is the creation of the capitalist class.

VON BERG, *in terrible mourning and anxiety*: But they adore him! My own cook, my gardeners, the people who work in my forests, the chauffeur, the gamekeeper—they are *Nazis*! I saw it coming over them, the love for this creature—my housekeeper dreams of him in her bed, she'd serve my breakfast like a god had slept with her; in a dream slicing my toast! I saw this adoration in my own house! That, that is the dreadful fact. *Controlling himself*: I beg your pardon, but it disturbs me. I admire your faith; all faith to some degree is beautiful. And when I know that yours is based on something so untrue—it's terribly disturbing. *Quietly*: In any case, I cannot glory in the facts; there is no reassurance there. They adore him, the salt of the earth. . . . *Staring*: Adore him.

*There is a burst of laughter from within the office.
He glances there, as they all do.*

Strange; if I did not know that some of them in there were
French, I'd have said they laugh like Germans. I suppose
vulgarity has no nation, after all.

*The door opens. Mr. Ferrand comes out, laughing;
within, the laughter is subsiding. He waves within,
closing the door. His smile drops. And as he goes past
the Waiter, he glances back at the door, then quickly
leans over and whispers hurriedly into his ear. They
all watch. Now Ferrand starts away. The Waiter
reaches out and grasps his apron.*

WAITER: Ferrand!

FERRAND, *brushing the Waiter's hand off his apron*: What
can I do? I told you fifty times to get out of this city! Didn't
I? *Starting to weep*: Didn't I?

*He hurries up the corridor, wiping his tears with his
apron. They all watch the Waiter, who sits there
staring.*

BAYARD: What? Tell me. Come on, I'm next, what'd he say?

WAITER—*whispers, staring ahead in shock*: It's not to work.

LEDUC, *leaning over toward him to hear*: What?

WAITER: They have furnaces.

BAYARD: What furnaces? . . . Talk! What is it?

WAITER: He heard the detectives; they came in for coffee
just before. People get burned up in furnaces. It's not to
work. They burn you up in Poland.

Silence. A long moment passes.

MONCEAU: That is the most fantastic idiocy I ever heard in my life!

LEBEAU, *to the Waiter*: As long as you have regular French papers, though . . . There's nothing about Jew on *my* papers.

WAITER, *in a loud whisper*: They're going to look at your penis.

> *The Boy stands up as though with an electric shock. The door of the office opens; the Police Captain appears and beckons to Bayard. The Boy quickly sits.*

CAPTAIN: You can come now.

> *Bayard stands, assuming an artificial and almost absurd posture of confidence. But approaching the Captain he achieves an authority.*

BAYARD: I'm a master electrician with the railroad, Captain. You may have seen me there. I'm classified First Priority War Worker.

CAPTAIN: Inside.

BAYARD: You can check with Transport Minister Duquesne.

CAPTAIN: You telling me my business?

BAYARD: No, but we can all use advice from time to time.

CAPTAIN: Inside.

BAYARD: Right.

> *Without hesitation Bayard walks into the office, the Captain following and closing the door.*

A long silence. Monceau, after a moment, smooths out a rough place on the felt of his hat. Lebeau looks at his papers, slowly rubbing his beard with the back of his hand, staring in terror. The Old Jew draws his bundle deeper under his feet. Leduc takes out a nearly empty pack of cigarettes, starts to take one for himself, then silently stands, crosses the line of men, and offers it to them. Lebeau takes one.

They light up. Faintly, from the next-door building, an accordion is heard playing a popular tune.

LEBEAU: Leave it to a cop to play now.

WAITER: No, that's the boss's son, Maurice. They're starting to serve lunch.

Leduc, who has returned to his position as the last man on the bench, cranes around the corner of the corridor, observes, and sits back.

LEDUC, *quietly*: There's only one guard at the door. Three men could take him.

Pause. No one responds. Then . . .

VON BERG, *apologetically*: I'm afraid I'd only get in your way. I have no strength in my hands.

MONCEAU, *to Leduc*: You actually believe that, Doctor? About the furnaces?

LEDUC—*he thinks*; *then*: I believe it is possible, yes. Come, we can do something.

MONCEAU: But what good are dead Jews to them? They want free labor. It's senseless. You can say whatever you like, but the Germans are not illogical; there's no conceivable advantage for them in such a thing.

LEDUC: You can be sitting here and still speak of advantages? Is there a rational explanation for your sitting here? But you are sitting here, aren't you?

MONCEAU: But an atrocity like that is . . . beyond any belief.

VON BERG: That is exactly the point.

MONCEAU: *You* don't believe it. Prince, you can't tell me you believe such a thing.

VON BERG: I find it the most believable atrocity I have heard.

LEBEAU: But why?

Slight pause.

VON BERG: Because it *is* so inconceivably vile. That is their power. To do the inconceivable; it paralyzes the rest of us. But if that is its purpose it is not the cause. Many times I used to ask my friends—if you love your country why is it necessary to hate other countries? To be a good German why must you despise everything that is not German? Until I realized the answer. They do these things not because they are German but because they are nothing. It is the hallmark of the age—the less you exist the more important it is to make a clear impression. I can see them discussing it as a kind of . . . truthfulness. After all, what *is* self-restraint but hypocrisy? If you despise Jews the most honest thing is to burn them up. And the fact that it costs money, and uses up trains and personnel—this only guarantees the integrity, the purity, the existence of their feelings. They would even tell you that only a Jew would think of the cost. They are poets, they are striving for a new nobility, the nobility of the totally vulgar. I believe in this fire; it would prove for all time that they exist, yes, and that they were sincere. You must not calculate these people with some nineteenth-century arithmetic of loss and gain. Their motives are musical, and people are merely sounds they play. And in my opinion, win or lose this war, they have pointed the way to the future. What one used to conceive a human being to be will have no room on this earth. I would try anything to get out.

> *A pause.*

MONCEAU: But they arrested you. That German professor is an expert. There is nothing Jewish about you. . . .

VON BERG: I have an accent. I noticed he reacted when I started to speak. It is an Austrian inflection. He may think I am another refugee.

> *The door opens. The Professor comes out, and indicates the Waiter.*

PROFESSOR: Next. You.

> *The Waiter makes himself small, pressing up against Lebeau.*

Don't be alarmed, it's only to check your papers.

> *The Waiter suddenly bends over and runs away— around the corner and up the corridor. The Guard appears at the end, collars him, and walks him back down the corridor.*

WAITER, *to the Guard*: Felix, you know me. Felix, my wife will go crazy. Felix . . .

PROFESSOR: Take him in the office.

> *The Police Captain appears in the office doorway.*

GUARD: There's nobody at the door.

CAPTAIN—*grabs the Waiter from the Guard*: Get in here, you Jew son-of-a-bitch. . . .

> *He throws the Waiter into the office; the Waiter collides with the Major, who is just coming out to see what the disturbance is. The Major grips his thigh in pain, pushing the Waiter clear. The Waiter slides to the Major's feet, weeping pleadingly. The Captain strides over and violently jerks him to his feet and pushes him into the office, going in after him.*
>
> *From within, unseen:*

You want trouble? You want trouble?

> *The Waiter is heard crying out; there is the sound of blows struck. Quiet. The Professor starts toward the door. The Major takes his arm and leads him down to the extreme forward edge of the stage, out of hearing of the prisoners.*

MAJOR: Wouldn't it be much simpler if they were just asked whether they . . .

> *Impatiently, without replying, the Professor goes over to the line of prisoners.*

PROFESSOR: Will any of you admit right now that you are carrying forged identification papers?

> *Silence.*

So. In short, you are all bona fide Frenchmen.

> *Silence. He goes over to the Old Jew, bends into his face.*

Are there any Jews among you?

Silence. Then he returns to the Major.

There's the problem, Major; either we go house by house investigating everyone's biography, or we make this inspection.

MAJOR: That electrician fellow just now, though—I thought he made a point there. In fact, only this morning in the hospital, while I was waiting my turn for X-ray, another officer, a German officer, a captain, in fact—his bathrobe happened to fall open . . .

PROFESSOR: It is entirely possible.

MAJOR: It was unmistakable, Professor.

PROFESSOR: Let us be clear, Major; the Race Institute does not claim that circumcision is conclusive proof of Jewish blood. The Race Institute recognizes that a small proportion of gentiles . . .

MAJOR: I don't see any reason not to say it, Professor—I happen to be, myself.

PROFESSOR: Very well, but I certainly would never mistake you for a Jew. Any more than you could mistake a pig for a horse. Science is not capricious, Major; my degree is in racial anthropology. In any case, we can certainly separate the gentiles by this kind of examination.

He has taken the Major's arm to lead him back to the office.

MAJOR: Excuse me. I'll be back in a few minutes. *Moving to leave*: You can carry on without me.

PROFESSOR: Major; you have your orders; you are in command of this operation. I must insist you take your place beside me.

MAJOR: I think some mistake has been made. I am a line officer, I have no experience with things of this kind. My training is engineering and artillery.

Slight pause.

PROFESSOR—*he speaks more quietly, his eyes ablaze*: We'd better be candid, Major. Are you refusing this assignment?

MAJOR, *registering the threat he feels*: I'm in pain today, Professor. They are still removing fragments. In fact, I understood I was only to . . . hold this desk down until an S.S. officer took over. I'm more or less on loan, you see, from the regular Army.

PROFESSOR—*takes his arm, draws him down to the edge of the stage again*: But the Army is not exempt from carrying out the Racial Program. My orders come from the top. And my report will go to the top. You understand me.

MAJOR—*his resistance seems to fall*: I do, yes.

PROFESSOR: Look now, if you wish to be relieved, I can easily telephone General von—

MAJOR: No—no, that's all right. I . . . I'll be back in a few minutes.

PROFESSOR: This is bizarre, Major—how long am I supposed to wait for you?

MAJOR, *holding back an outburst of resentment*: I need a walk. I am not used to sitting in an office. I see nothing bizarre in it, I am a line officer, and this kind of business takes a little getting used to. *Through his teeth*: What do you find bizarre in it?

PROFESSOR: Very well.

Slight pause.

MAJOR: I'll be back in ten minutes. You can carry on.

PROFESSOR: I will not continue without you, Major. The Army's responsibility is quite as great as mine here.

MAJOR: I won't be long.

> *The Professor turns abruptly and strides into the office, slamming the door shut. Very much wanting to get out, the Major goes up the corridor. Leduc stands as he passes.*

LEDUC: Major . . .

> *The Major limps past him without turning, up the corridor and out. Silence.*

BOY: Mister?

> *Leduc turns to him.*

I'd try it with you.

LEDUC, *to Monceau and Lebeau*: What about you two?

LEBEAU: Whatever you say, but I'm so hungry I wouldn't do you much good.

LEDUC: You can walk up to him and start an argument. Distract his attention. Then we—

MONCEAU: You're both crazy, they'll shoot you down.

LEDUC: Some of us might make it. There's only one man at the door. This neighborhood is full of alleyways—you could disappear in twenty yards.

MONCEAU: How long would you be free—an hour? And when they catch you they'll really tear you apart.

BOY: Please! I have to get out. I was on my way to the pawnshop. *Takes out a ring.* It's my mother's wedding ring, it's all that's left. She's waiting for the money. They have nothing in the house to eat.

MONCEAU: You take my advice, boy; don't do anything, they'll let you go.

LEDUC: Like the electrician?

MONCEAU: He was obviously a Communist. And the waiter irritated the Captain.

LEBEAU: Look, I'll try it with you but don't expect too much; I'm weak as a chicken, I haven't eaten since yesterday.

LEDUC, *to Monceau*: It would be better with another man. The boy is very light. If you and the boy rush him I'll get his gun away.

VON BERG, *to Leduc, looking at his hands*: Forgive me.

Monceau springs up, goes to a box, and sits.

MONCEAU: I am not going to risk my life for nothing. That businessman had a Jewish face. *To Lebeau*: You said so yourself.

LEBEAU, *to Leduc, appeasingly*: I did. I thought so. Look, if your papers are good, maybe that's it.

LEDUC, *to Lebeau and Monceau*: You know yourself the Germans have been moving into the Southern Zone; you see they are picking up Jews; a man has just told you that you are marked for destruction. . . .

MONCEAU—*indicates Von Berg*: They took him in. Nobody's explained it.

VON BERG: My accent . . .

MONCEAU: My dear Prince, only an idiot could mistake you for anything but an Austrian of the upper class. I took you for nobility the minute you walked in.

LEDUC: But if it's a general checkup why would they be looking at penises?

MONCEAU: There's no evidence of that!

LEDUC: The waiter's boss . . .

MONCEAU, *suppressing a nervous shout*: He overheard two French detectives who can't possibly know anything about what happens in Poland. And if they do that kind of thing, it's not the end either—I had Jew stamped on my passport in Paris and I was playing Cyrano at the same time.

VON BERG: Really! Cyrano!

LEBEAU: Then why'd you leave Paris?

MONCEAU: It was an absolutely idiotic accident. I was rooming with another actor, a gentile. And he kept warning me to get out. But naturally one doesn't just give up a role like that. But one night I let myself be influenced by him. He pointed out that I had a number of books which were on the forbidden list—of Communist literature—I mean things like Sinclair Lewis, and Thomas Mann, and even a few things by Friedrich Engels, which everybody was reading at one time. And I decided I might as well get rid of them. So we made bundles and I lived on the fifth floor of a walkup and we'd take turns going down to the street and just leaving them on benches or in doorways or anywhere at all. It was after midnight, and I was just dropping a bundle into the gutter near the Opéra, when I noticed a man standing in a doorway watching me. At that moment I realized that I had stamped my name and address in every one of those books.

VON BERG: Hah! What did you do?

MONCEAU: Started walking, and kept right on down here to the Unoccupied Zone. *An outcry of remorse*: But in my opinion, if I'd done nothing at all I might still be working!

LEDUC, *with higher urgency, but deeply sympathetic; to Monceau*: Listen to me for one moment. I beg you. There is only one man guarding that door; we may never get another chance like this again.

LEBEAU: That's another thing; if it was all that serious, wouldn't they be guarding us more heavily? I mean, that's a point.

LEDUC: That is exactly the point. They are relying on us.

MONCEAU: Relying on us!

LEDUC: Yes. To project our own reasonable ideas into their heads. It is reasonable that a light guard means the thing is not important. They rely on our own logic to immobilize ourselves. But you have just told us how you went all over Paris advertising the fact that you owned forbidden books.

MONCEAU: But I didn't do it purposely.

LEDUC: May I guess that you could no longer bear the tension of remaining in Paris? But that you wanted to keep your role in Cyrano and had to find some absolute compulsion to save your own life? It was your unconscious mind that saved you. Do you understand? You cannot wager your life on a purely rational analysis of this situation. Listen to your feelings; you must certainly *feel* the danger here. . . .

MONCEAU, *in high anxiety*: I played in Germany. That audience could not burn up actors in a furnace. *Turning to Von Berg*: Prince, you cannot tell me you believe that!

VON BERG, *after a pause*: I supported a small orchestra. When the Germans came into Austria three of the players prepared to escape. I convinced them no harm would come to them; I brought them to my castle; we all lived together. The oboist was twenty, twenty-one—the heart stopped when he played certain tones. They came for him in the garden. They took him out of his chair. The instrument lay on the lawn like a dead bone. I made certain inquiries; he is dead now. And it was even more terrible—they came and sat down and listened until the rehearsal was over. And *then* they took him. It is as though they wished to take him at exactly the moment when he was most beautiful. I know how you feel—but I tell you nothing any longer is forbidden. Nothing. *Tears are in his eyes; he turns to Leduc.* I ask you to forgive me, Doctor.

> *Pause.*

BOY: Will they let you go?

VON BERG, *with a guilty glance at the Boy*: I suppose. If this is all to catch Jews they will let me go.

BOY: Would you take this ring? And bring it back to my mother?

> *He stretches his hand out with the ring. Von Berg does not touch it.*

Number Nine Rue Charlot. Top floor. Hirsch. Sarah Hirsch. She has long brown hair . . . be sure it's her. She has a little beauty mark on this cheek. There are two other families in the apartment, so be sure it's her.

> *Von Berg looks into the Boy's face. Silence. Then he turns to Leduc.*

VON BERG: Come. Tell me what to do. I'll try to help you. *To Leduc*: Doctor?

LEDUC: I'm afraid it's hopeless.

VON BERG: Why?

LEDUC—*stares ahead, then looks at Lebeau*: He's weak with hunger, and the boy's like a feather. I wanted to get away, not just slaughtered. *Pause. With bitter irony*: I live in the country, you see; I haven't talked to anybody in so long, I'm afraid I came in here with the wrong assumptions.

MONCEAU: If you're trying to bait me, Doctor, forget it.

LEDUC: Would you mind telling me, are you religious?

MONCEAU: Not at all.

LEDUC: Then why do you feel this desire to be sacrificed?

MONCEAU: I ask you to stop talking to me.

LEDUC: But you are making a gift of yourself. You are the only able-bodied man here, aside from me, and yet you feel no impulse to do something? I don't understand your air of confidence.

    Pause.

MONCEAU: I refuse to play a part I do not fit. Everyone is playing the victim these days; hopeless, hysterical, they always assume the worst. I have papers; I will present them with the single idea that they must be honored. I think that is exactly what saved that businessman. You accuse us of acting the part the Germans created for us; I think you're the one who's doing that by acting so desperate.

LEDUC: And if, despite your act, they throw you into a freight car?

MONCEAU: I don't think they will.

LEDUC: But if they do. You certainly have enough imagination to visualize that.

MONCEAU: In that case, I will have done my best. I know what failure is; it took me a long time to make good; I haven't the personality for leading roles; everyone said I was crazy to stay in the profession. But I did, and I imposed my idea on others.

LEDUC: In other words, you will create yourself.

MONCEAU: Every actor creates himself.

LEDUC: But when they tell you to open your fly.

Monceau is silent, furious.

Please don't stop now; I'm very interested. How do you regard that moment?

Monceau is silent.

Believe me, I am only trying to understand this. I am incapable of penetrating such passivity; I ask you what is in your mind when you face the command to open your fly. I am being as impersonal, as scientific as I know how to be— I believe I am going to be murdered. What do you believe will happen when they point to that spot between your legs?

Pause.

MONCEAU: I have nothing to say to you.

LEBEAU: I'll tell you what I'll feel. *Indicates Von Berg.* I'll wish I was him.

LEDUC: To be someone else.

LEBEAU, *exhausted*: Yes. To have been arrested by mistake. God—to see them relaxing when they realize I am innocent.

LEDUC: You feel guilty, then.

LEBEAU—*he has gradually become closer to exhaustion*: A little, I guess. Not for anything I've done but . . . I don't know why.

LEDUC: For being a Jew, perhaps?

LEBEAU: I'm not ashamed of being a Jew.

LEDUC: Then why feel guilty?

LEBEAU: I don't know. Maybe it's that they keep saying such terrible things about us, and you can't answer. And after years and years of it, you . . . I wouldn't say you believe it, but . . . you do, a little. It's a funny thing—I used to say to my mother and father just what you're saying. We could have gone to America a month before the invasion. But they wouldn't leave Paris. She had this brass bed, and carpets, and draperies and all kinds of junk. Like him with his Cyrano. And I told them, "You're doing just what they want you to do!" But, see, people won't believe they can be killed. Not them with their brass bed and their carpets and their faces. . . .

LEDUC: But do you believe it? It seems to me you don't believe it yourself.

LEBEAU: I believe it. They only caught me this morning because I . . . I always used to walk in the morning before I sat down to work. And I wanted to do it again. I knew I shouldn't go outside. But you get tired of believing in the truth. You get tired of seeing things clearly. *Pause.* I always collected my illusions in the morning. I could never paint what I saw, only what I imagined. And this morning, danger or no danger, I just had to get out, to walk around, to see something real, something else but the inside of my head . . . and I hardly turned the corner and that motherless son-of-a-bitch of a scientist got out of the car with his fingers going for my nose. . . . *Pause.* I believe I can die. But you can get so tired . . .

LEDUC: That it's not too bad.

LEBEAU: Almost, yes.

LEDUC, *glancing at them all*: So that one way or the other, with illusions or without them, exhausted or fresh—we have been trained to die. The Jew and the gentile both.

MONCEAU: You're still trying to bait me, Doctor, but if you want to commit suicide do it alone, don't involve others. The fact is there are laws and every government enforces its laws; and I want it understood that I have nothing to do with any of this talk.

LEDUC, *angering now*: Every government does not have laws condemning people because of their race.

MONCEAU: I beg your pardon. The Russians condemn the middle class, the English have condemned the Indians, Africans, and anybody else they could lay their hands on, the French, the Italians . . . every nation has condemned somebody because of his race, including the Americans and what they do to Negroes. The vast majority of mankind is condemned because of its race. What do you advise all these people—suicide?

LEDUC: What do you advise?

MONCEAU, *seeking and finding conviction*: I go on the assumption that if I obey the law with dignity I will live in peace. I may not like the law, but evidently the majority does, or they would overthrow it. And I'm speaking now of the French majority, who outnumber the Germans in this town fifty to one. These are French police, don't forget, not German. And if by some miracle you did knock out that guard you would find yourself in a city where not one person in a thousand would help you. And it's got nothing to do with being Jewish or not Jewish. It is what the world is, so why don't you stop insulting others with romantic challenges!

LEDUC: In short, because the world is indifferent you will wait calmly and with great dignity—to open your fly.

MONCEAU—*frightened and furious, he stands*: I'll tell you what I think; I think it's people like you who brought this on us. People who give Jews a reputation for subversion, and this Talmudic analysis, and this everlasting, niggling discontent.

LEDUC: Then I will tell you that I was wrong before; you didn't advertise your name on those forbidden books in order to find a reason to leave Paris and save yourself. It was in order to get yourself caught and be put out of your misery. Your heart is conquered territory, mister.

MONCEAU: If we meet again you will pay for that remark.

LEDUC: Conquered territory! *He leans forward, his head in his hands.*

BOY, *reaching over to hand the ring to Von Berg*: Will you do it? Number nine Rue Charlot?

VON BERG, *deeply affected*: I will try.

> *He takes the ring. The Boy immediately stands.*

LEDUC: Where are you going?

The Boy, terrified but desperate, moves on the balls of his feet to the corridor and peeks around the corner. Leduc stands, tries to draw him back.

You can't; it'll take three men to . . .

The boy shakes loose and walks rapidly up the hallway. Leduc hesitates, then goes after him.

Wait! Wait a minute! I'm coming.

The Major enters the corridor at its far end. The Boy halts, Leduc now beside him. For a moment they stand facing him. Then they turn and come down the corridor and sit, the Major following them. He touches Leduc's sleeve, and Leduc stands and follows him downstage.

MAJOR—*he is "high"—with drink and a flow of emotion*: That's impossible. Don't try it. There are sentries on both corners. *Glancing toward the office door*: Captain, I would only like to say that . . . this is all as inconceivable to me as it is to you. Can you believe that?

LEDUC: I'd believe it if you shot yourself. And better yet, if you took a few of them with you.

MAJOR, *wiping his mouth with the back of his hand*: We would all be replaced by tomorrow morning, wouldn't we?

LEDUC: We might get out alive, though; you could see to that.

MAJOR: They'd find you soon.

LEDUC: Not me.

MAJOR, *with a manic amusement, yet deeply questioning*: Why do you deserve to live more than I do?

LEDUC: Because I am incapable of doing what you are doing. I am better for the world than you.

MAJOR: It means nothing to you that I have feelings about this?

LEDUC: Nothing whatever, unless you get us out of here.

MAJOR: And then what? Then what?

LEDUC: I will remember a decent German, an honorable German.

MAJOR: Will that make a difference?

LEDUC: I will love you as long as I live. Will anyone do that now?

MAJOR: That means so much to you—that someone love you?

LEDUC: That I be worthy of someone's love, yes. And respect.

MAJOR: It's amazing; you don't understand anything. Nothing of that kind is left, don't you understand that yet?

LEDUC: It is left in me.

MAJOR, *more loudly, a fury rising in him*: There are no persons any more, don't you see that? There will never be persons again. What do I care if you love me? Are you out of your mind? What am I, a dog that I must be loved? You— *turning to all of them*—goddamned Jews!

> *The door opens; the Professor and the Police Captain appear.*

Like dogs, Jew-dogs. Look at him—*indicating the Old Jew*—with his paws folded. Look what happens when I yell at him. Dog! He doesn't move. Does he move? Do you see him moving? *He strides to the Professor and takes him by the arm.* But we move, don't we? We measure your noses, don't we, Herr Professor, and we look at your cocks, we keep moving continually!

PROFESSOR, *with a gesture to draw him inside*: Major . . .

MAJOR: Hands off, you civilian bastard.

PROFESSOR: I think . . .

MAJOR, *drawing his revolver*: Not a word!

PROFESSOR: You're drunk.

> *The Major fires into the ceiling. The prisoners tense in shock.*

MAJOR: Everything stops now.

> *He goes in thought, revolver cocked in his hand, and sits beside Lebeau.*

Now it is all stopped.

> *His hands are shaking. He sniffs in his running nose. He crosses his legs to control them, and looks at Leduc, who is still standing.*

Now you tell me. You tell me. Now nothing is moving. You tell me. Go ahead now.

LEDUC: What shall I tell you?

MAJOR: Tell me how . . . how there can be persons any more. I have you at the end of this revolver—*indicates the Professor*—he has me—and somebody has him—and somebody has somebody else. Now tell me.

LEDUC: I told you.

MAJOR: I won't repeat it. I am a man of honor. What do you make of that? I will not tell them what you advised me to do. What do you say—damned decent of me, isn't it . . . not to repeat your advice?

> *Leduc is silent. The Major gets up, comes to Leduc. Pause.*

You are a combat veteran.

LEDUC: Yes.

MAJOR: No record of subversive activities against the German authority.

LEDUC: No.

MAJOR: If you were released, and the others were kept . . . would you refuse?

> *Leduc starts to turn away. The Major nudges him with the pistol, forcing him face to face.*

Would you refuse?

LEDUC: No.

MAJOR: And walk out of that door with a light heart?

LEDUC—*he is looking at the floor now*: I don't know. *He starts to put his trembling hands into his pockets.*

MAJOR: Don't hide your hands. I am trying to understand why you are better for the world than me. Why do you hide your hands? Would you go out that door with a light heart, run to your woman, drink a toast to your skin? . . . Why are you better than anybody else?

LEDUC: I have no duty to make a gift of myself to your sadism.

MAJOR: But I do? To others' sadism? Of myself? I have that duty and you do not? To make a gift of myself?

LEDUC—*looks at the Professor and the Police Captain, glances back at the Major*: I have nothing to say.

MAJOR: That's better.

> *He suddenly gives Leduc an almost comradely push and nearly laughs. He puts his gun away, turns swaying to the Professor and with a victorious shout*:

Next!

> *The Major brushes past the Professor into the office. Lebeau has not moved.*

PROFESSOR: This way.

> *Lebeau stands up, starts sleepily toward the corridor, turns about, and moves into the office, the Professor following him.*

CAPTAIN, *to Leduc*: Get back there.

> *Leduc returns to his seat. The Captain goes into the office; the door shuts. Pause.*

MONCEAU: You happy now? You got him furious. You happy?

> *The door opens; the Captain appears, beckoning to Monceau.*

CAPTAIN: Next.

Monceau gets up at once; taking papers out of his jacket, he fixes a smile on his face and walks with erect elegance to the Captain and with a slight bow, his voice cheerful:

MONCEAU: Good morning, Captain.

He goes right into the office; the Captain follows, and shuts the door. Pause.

BOY: Number nine Rue Charlot. Please.

VON BERG: I'll give it to her.

BOY: I'm a minor. I'm not even fifteen. Does it apply to minors?

Captain opens the door, beckons to the Boy.

BOY, *standing*: I'm a minor. I'm not fifteen until February . . .

CAPTAIN: Inside.

BOY, *halting before the Captain*: I could get my birth certificate for you.

CAPTAIN, *prodding him along*: Inside, inside.

They go in. The door shuts. The accordion is heard again from next door. The Old Jew begins to rock back and forth slightly, praying softly. Von Berg, his hand trembling as it passes down his cheek, stares at the Old Jew, then turns to Leduc on his other side. The three are alone now.

VON BERG: Does he realize what is happening?

LEDUC, *with an edgy note of impatience*: As much as anyone can, I suppose.

VON BERG: He seems to be watching it all from the stars. *Slight pause.* I wish we could have met under other circumstances. There are a great many things I'd like to have asked you.

LEDUC, *rapidly, sensing the imminent summons*: I'd appreciate it if you'd do me a favor.

VON BERG: Certainly.

LEDUC: Will you go and tell my wife?

VON BERG: Where is she?

LEDUC: Take the main highway north two kilometers. You'll see a small forest on the left and a dirt road leading into it. Go about a kilometer until you see the river. Follow the river to a small mill. They are in the tool shed behind the wheel.

VON BERG, *distressed*: And . . . what shall I say?

LEDUC: That I've been arrested. And that there may be a possibility I can . . . *Breaks off.* No, tell her the truth.

VON BERG, *alarmed*: What do you mean?

LEDUC: The furnaces. Tell her that.

VON BERG: But actually . . . that's only a rumor, isn't it?

LEDUC—*turns to him—sharply*: I don't regard it as a rumor. It should be known. I never heard of it before. It must be known. Just take her aside—there's no need for the children to hear it, but tell her.

VON BERG: It's only that it would be difficult for me. To tell such a thing to a woman.

LEDUC: If it's happening you can find a way to say it, can't you?

VON BERG—*hesitates; he senses Leduc's resentment*: Very well. I'll tell her. It's only that I have no great . . . facility with women. But I'll do as you say. *Pause. He glances to the door.* They're taking longer with that boy. Maybe he *is* too young, you suppose?

> *Leduc does not answer. Von Berg seems suddenly hopeful.*

They would stick to the rules, you know. . . . In fact, with the shortage of physicians you suppose they—

> *He breaks off.*

I'm sorry if I said anything to offend you.

LEDUC, *struggling with his anger*: That's all right.

> *Slight pause. His voice is trembling with anger.*

It's just that you keep finding these little shreds of hope and it's a little difficult.

VON BERG: Yes, I see. I beg your pardon. I understand.

> *Pause. Leduc glances at the door; he is shifting about in high tension.*

Would you like to talk of something else, perhaps? Are you interested in . . . in music?

LEDUC, *desperately trying to control himself*: It's really quite simple. It's that you'll survive, you see.

VON BERG: But I can't help that, can I?

LEDUC: That only makes it worse! I'm sorry, one isn't always in control of one's emotions.

VON BERG: Doctor, I can promise you—it will not be easy for me to walk out of here. You don't know me.

LEDUC—*he tries not to reply; then*: I'm afraid it will only be difficult because it is so easy.

VON BERG: I think that's unfair.

LEDUC: Well, it doesn't matter.

VON BERG: It does to me. I . . . I can tell you that I was very close to suicide in Austria. Actually, that is why I left. When they murdered my musicians—not that alone, but when I told the story to many of my friends there was hardly any reaction. That was almost worse. Do you understand such indifference?

LEDUC—*he seems on the verge of an outbreak*: You have a curious idea of human nature. It's astounding you can go on with it in these times.

VON BERG, *with hand on heart*: But what is left if one gives up one's ideals? What *is* there?

LEDUC: Who are you talking about? You? Or me?

VON BERG: I'm terribly sorry. . . . I understand.

LEDUC: Why don't you just stop talking. I can't listen to anything. *Slight pause*. Forgive me. I do appreciate your feeling. *Slight pause*. I see it too clearly, perhaps—I know the violence inside these people's heads. It's difficult to listen to amelioration, even if it's well-meant.

VON BERG: I had no intention of ameliorating—

LEDUC: I think you do. And you must; you will survive, you will have to ameliorate it; just a little, just enough. It's no reflection on you. *Slight pause*. But, you see, this is why one gets so furious. Because all this suffering is so pointless— it can never be a lesson, it can never have a meaning. And that is why it will be repeated again and again forever.

Von Berg: Because it cannot be shared?

Leduc: Yes. Because it cannot be shared. It is total, absolute, waste.

> *He leans forward suddenly, trying to collect himself against his terror. He glances at the door.*

How strange—one can even become impatient.

> *A groan as he shakes his head with wonder and anger at himself.*

Hm!—what devils they are.

Von Berg, *with an overtone of closeness to Leduc*: You understand now why I left Vienna. They can make death seductive. It is their worst sin. I had dreams at night—Hitler in a great flowing cloak, almost like a gown, almost like a woman. He was beautiful.

Leduc: Listen—don't mention the furnaces to my wife.

Von Berg: I'm glad you say that, I feel very relieved, there's really no point . . .

Leduc, *in a higher agony as he realizes*: No, it's . . . it's . . . You see there was no reason for me to be caught here. We have a good hideout. They'd never have found us. But she has an exposed nerve in one tooth and I thought I might find some codein. Just say I was arrested.

Von Berg: Does she have sufficient money?

Leduc: You could help her that way if you like. Thank you.

Von Berg: The children are small?

Leduc: Two and three.

VON BERG: How dreadful. How dreadful. *He looks with a glance of fury at the door.* Do you suppose if I offered him something? I can get hold of a good deal of money. I know so little about people—I'm afraid he's rather an idealist. It could infuriate him more.

LEDUC: You might try to feel him out. I don't know what to tell you.

VON BERG: How upside down everything is—to find oneself wishing for a money-loving cynic!

LEDUC: It's perfectly natural. We have learned the price of idealism.

VON BERG: And yet can one wish for a world without ideals? That's what's so depressing—one doesn't know what to wish for.

LEDUC, *in anger*: You see, I knew it when I walked down the road, I knew it was senseless! For a goddamned toothache! So what, so she doesn't sleep for a couple of weeks! It was perfectly clear I shouldn't be taking the chance.

VON BERG: Yes, but if one loves someone . . .

LEDUC: We are not in love any more. It's just too difficult to separate in these times.

VON BERG: Oh, how terrible.

LEDUC, *more softly, realizing a new idea*: Listen . . . about the furnaces . . . don't mention that to her. Not a word, please. *With great self-contempt*: God, at a time like this— to think of taking vengeance on her! What scum we are! *He almost sways in despair.*

> Pause. Von Berg turns to Leduc; tears are in his eyes.

VON BERG: There is nothing, is that it? For you there is nothing?

LEDUC, *flying out at him suddenly*: Well what do you propose? Excuse me, but what in hell are you talking about?

> *The door opens. The Professor comes out and beckons to the Old Jew. He seems upset, by an argument he had in the office, possibly.*

Next.

> *The Old Jew does not turn to him.*

You hear me, why do you sit there?

> *He strides to the Old Jew and lifts him to his feet brusquely. The man reaches down to pick up his bundle, but the Professor tries to push it back to the floor.*

Leave that.

> *With a wordless little cry, the Old Jew clings to his bundle.*

Leave it!

> *The Professor strikes at the Old Jew's hand, but he only holds on tighter, uttering his wordless little cries. The Police Captain comes out as the Professor pulls at the bundle.*

Let go of that!

> *The bundle rips open. A white cloud of feathers blows up out of it. For an instant everything stops as the Professor looks in surprise at the feathers floating down. The Major appears in the doorway as the feathers settle.*

CAPTAIN: Come on.

> *The Captain and the Professor lift the Old Jew and carry him past the Major into the office. The Major with deadened eyes glances at the feathers and limps in, closing the door behind him.*
>
> *Leduc and Von Berg stare at the feathers, some of which have fallen on them. They silently brush them off. Leduc picks the last one off his jacket, opens his fingers, and lets it fall to the floor.*
>
> *Silence. Suddenly a short burst of laughter is heard from the office.*

VON BERG, *with great difficulty, not looking at Leduc*: I would like to be able to part with your friendship. Is that possible?

> *Pause.*

LEDUC: Prince, in my profession one gets the habit of looking at oneself quite impersonally. It is not you I am angry with. In one part of my mind it is not even this Nazi. I am only angry that I should have been born before the day when man has accepted his own nature; that he is *not* reasonable, that he is full of murder, that his ideals are only the little tax he pays for the right to hate and kill with a clear conscience. I am only angry that, knowing this, I still deluded myself. That there was not time to truly make part of myself what I know, and to teach others the truth.

VON BERG, *angered, above his anxiety*: There are ideals, Doctor, of another kind. There are people who would find it easier to die than stain one finger with this murder. They exist. I swear it to you. People for whom everything is *not* permitted, foolish people and ineffectual, but they do exist and will not dishonor their tradition. *Desperately*: I ask your friendship.

> *Again laughter is heard from within the office. This time it is louder. Leduc slowly turns to Von Berg.*

LEDUC: I owe you the truth, Prince; you won't believe it now, but I wish you would think about it and what it means. I have never analyzed a gentile who did not have, somewhere hidden in his mind, a dislike if not a hatred for the Jews.

VON BERG, *clapping his ears shut, springing up*: That is impossible, it is not true of me!

LEDUC, *standing, coming to him, a wild pity in his voice*: Until you know it is true of you you will destroy whatever truth can come of this atrocity. Part of knowing who we are is knowing we are not someone else. And Jew is only the name we give to that stranger, that agony we cannot feel, that death we look at like a cold abstraction. Each man has his Jew; it is the other. And the Jews have their Jews. And now, now above all, you must see that you have yours—the man whose death leaves you relieved that you are not him, despite your decency. And that is why there is nothing and will be nothing—until you face your own complicity with this . . . your own humanity.

VON BERG: I deny that. I deny that absolutely. I have never in my life said a word against your people. Is that your implication? That I have something to do with this monstrousness! I have put a pistol to my head! To my head!

> *Laughter is heard again.*

LEDUC, *hopelessly*: I'm sorry; it doesn't really matter.

VON BERG: It matters very much to me. Very much to me!

LEDUC, *in a level tone full of mourning; and yet behind it a howling horror*: Prince, you asked me before if I knew your cousin, Baron Kessler.

Von Berg looks at him, already with anxiety.

Baron Kessler is a Nazi. He helped to remove all the Jewish doctors from the medical school.

Von Berg is struck; his eyes glance about.

You were aware of that, weren't you?

Half-hysterical laughter comes from the office.

You must have heard that at some time or another, didn't you?

VON BERG, *stunned, inward-seeing*: Yes. I heard it. I . . . had forgotten it. You see, he was . . .

LEDUC: . . . Your cousin. I understand.

They are quite joined; and Leduc is mourning for the Prince as much as for himself, despite his anger.

And in any case, it is only a small part of Baron Kessler to you. I do understand it. But it is all of Baron Kessler to me. When you said his name it was with love; and I'm sure he must be a man of some kindness, with whom you can see eye to eye in many things. But when I hear that name I see a knife. You see now why I say there is nothing, and will be nothing, when even you cannot really put yourself in my place? Even you! And that is why your thoughts of suicide do not move me. It's not your guilt I want, it's your responsibility—that might have helped. Yes, if you had understood that Baron Kessler was in part, in some part, in some small and frightful part—doing your will. You might have done something then, with your standing, and your name and your decency, aside from shooting yourself!

VON BERG, *in full horror, his face upthrust, calling*: What can ever save us? *He covers his face with his hands.*

> *The door opens. The Professor comes out.*

PROFESSOR, *beckoning to the Prince*: Next.

> *Von Berg does not turn, but holds Leduc in his horrified, beseeching gaze. The Professor approaches the Prince.*

Come!

> *The Professor reaches down to take Von Berg's arm. Von Berg angrily brushes away his abhorrent hand.*

VON BERG: *Hände weg!*

> *The Professor retracts his hand, immobilized, surprised, and for a moment has no strength against his own recognition of authority. Von Berg turns back to Leduc, who glances up at him and smiles with warmth, then turns away.*
>
> *Von Berg turns toward the door and, reaching into his breast pocket for a wallet of papers, goes into the office. The Professor follows and closes the door.*
>
> *Alone, Leduc sits motionless. Now he begins the movements of the trapped; he swallows with difficulty, crosses and recrosses his legs. Now he is still again and bends over and cranes around the corner of the corridor to look for the guard. A movement of his foot stirs up feathers. The accordion is heard outside. He angrily kicks a feather off his foot. Now he makes a decision; he quickly reaches into his pocket, takes out a clasp knife, opens the blade, and*

begins to get to his feet, starting for the corridor.
The door opens and Von Berg comes out. In his
hand is a white pass. The door shuts behind him.
He is looking at the pass as he goes by Leduc, and
suddenly turns, walks back, and thrusts the pass into
Leduc's hand.

VON BERG, *in a strangely angered whisper, motioning him*
out: Take it! Go!

Von Berg sits quickly on the bench, taking out the
wedding ring. Leduc stares at him, a horrified look on
his face. Von Berg hands him the ring.

Number nine Rue Charlot. Go.

LEDUC, *in a desperate whisper*: What will happen to you?

VON BERG, *angrily waving him away*: Go, go!

Leduc backs away, his hands springing to cover his
eyes in the awareness of his own guilt.

LEDUC—*a plea in his voice*: I wasn't asking you to do this!
You don't owe me this!

VON BERG: Go!

Leduc, his eyes wide in awe and terror, suddenly
turns and strides up the corridor. At the end of it
the Guard appears, hearing his footsteps. He gives
the Guard the pass and disappears.
A long pause. The door opens. The Professor ap-
pears.

PROFESSOR: Ne— *He breaks off. Looks about, then, to Von*
Berg: Where's your pass?

Von Berg stares ahead. The Professor calls into the
office.

Man escaped!

He runs up the corridor, calling.

Man escaped! Man escaped!

The Police Captain rushes out of the office. Voices are heard outside calling orders. The accordion stops. The Major hurries out of the office. The Police Captain rushes past him.

CAPTAIN: What? *Glancing back at Von Berg, he realizes and rushes up the corridor, calling*: Who let him out! Find that man! What happened?

The voices outside are swept away by a siren going off. The Major has gone to the opening of the corridor, following the Police Captain. For a moment he remains looking up the corridor. All that can be heard now is the siren moving off in pursuit. It dies away, leaving the Major's rapid and excited breaths, angry breaths, incredulous breaths.

Now he turns slowly to Von Berg, who is staring straight ahead. Von Berg turns and faces him. Then he gets to his feet. The moment lengthens, and lengthens yet. A look of anguish and fury is stiffening the Major's face; he is closing his fists. They stand there, forever incomprehensible to one another, looking into each other's eyes.

At the head of the corridor four new men, prisoners, appear. Herded by the Detectives, they enter the detention room and sit on the bench, glancing about at the ceiling, the walls, the feathers on the floor, and the two men who are staring at each other so strangely.

The play was staged by Harold Clurman for the Repertory Theatre of Lincoln Center for the Performing Arts. It was first performed on December 3, 1964, at the ANTA–Washington Square Theatre, New York City.

The Cast

(In order of speaking)

Lebeau	Michael Strong
Bayard	Stanley Beck
Marchand	Paul Mann
Police Guard	C. Thomas Blackwell
Monceau	David J. Stewart
Gypsy	Harold Scott
Waiter	Jack Waltzer
Boy	Ira Lewis
Major	Hal Holbrook
First Detective	Alek Primrose
Old Jew	Will Lee
Second Detective	James Dukas
Leduc	Joseph Wiseman
Police Captain	James Greene
Von Berg	David Wayne
Professor Hoffman	Clinton Kimbrough
Ferrand	Graham Jarvis
Prisoners	Pierre Epstein, Stephen Peters, Tony Lo Bianco, John Vari

FOR THE BEST IN PAPERBACKS, LOOK FOR THE

In every corner of the world, on every subject under the sun, Penguin represents quality and variety—the very best in publishing today.

For complete information about books available from Penguin—including Puffins, Penguin Classics, and Arkana—and how to order them, write to us at the appropriate address below. Please note that for copyright reasons the selection of books varies from country to country.

In the United Kingdom: Please write to *Dept. JC, Penguin Books Ltd, FREEPOST, West Drayton, Middlesex UB7 0BR.*

If you have any difficulty in obtaining a title, please send your order with the correct money, plus ten percent for postage and packaging, to *P.O. Box No. 11, West Drayton, Middlesex UB7 0BR*

In the United States: Please write to *Consumer Sales, Penguin USA, P.O. Box 999, Dept. 17109, Bergenfield, New Jersey 07621-0120.* VISA and MasterCard holders call 1-800-253-6476 to order all Penguin titles

In Canada: Please write to *Penguin Books Canada Ltd, 10 Alcorn Avenue, Suite 300, Toronto, Ontario M4V 3B2*

In Australia: Please write to *Penguin Books Australia Ltd, P.O. Box 257, Ringwood, Victoria 3134*

In New Zealand: Please write to *Penguin Books (NZ) Ltd, Private Bag 102902, North Shore Mail Centre, Auckland 10*

In India: Please write to *Penguin Books India Pvt Ltd, 706 Eros Apartments, 56 Nehru Place, New Delhi 110 019*

In the Netherlands: Please write to *Penguin Books Netherlands bv, Postbus 3507, NL-1001 AH Amsterdam*

In Germany: Please write to *Penguin Books Deutschland GmbH, Metzlerstrasse 26, 60594 Frankfurt am Main*

In Spain: Please write to *Penguin Books S. A., Bravo Murillo 19, 1° B, 28015 Madrid*

In Italy: Please write to *Penguin Italia s.r.l., Via Felice Casati 20, I-20124 Milano*

In France: Please write to *Penguin France S. A., 17 rue Lejeune, F–31000 Toulouse*

In Japan: Please write to *Penguin Books Japan, Ishikiribashi Building, 2–5–4, Suido, Bunkyo-ku, Tokyo 112*

In Greece: Please write to *Penguin Hellas Ltd, Dimocritou 3, GR–106 71 Athens*

In South Africa: Please write to *Longman Penguin Southern Africa (Pty) Ltd, Private Bag X08, Bertsham 2013*